THE ELEMENTS OF STYLE

WILLIAM STRUNK, JR.

Originally published by

ITHACA, N.Y.: W.P. HUMPHREY

CONTENTS

3

I. INTRODUCTORY

This book aims to give in brief space the principal requirements of plain English style. It aims to lighten the task of instructor and student by concentrating attention (in Chapters II and III) on a few essentials, the rules of usage and principles of composition most commonly violated. In accordance with this plan it lays down three rules for the use of the comma, instead of a score or more, and one for the use of the semicolon, in the belief that these four rules provide for all the internal punctuation that is required by nineteen sentences out of twenty. Similarly, it gives in Chapter III only those principles of the paragraph and the sentence which are of the widest application. The book thus covers only a small portion of the field of English style. The experience of its writer has been that once past the essentials, students profit most by individual instruction based on the problems of their own work, and that each instructor has his own body of theory, which he may prefer to that offered by any textbook.

The numbers of the sections may be used as references in correcting manuscript.

The writer's colleagues in the Department of English in Cornell University have greatly helped him in the preparation of his manuscript Mr. George McLane Wood has kindly consented to the inclusion under Rule 10 of some material from his *Suggestions to Authors.*

The following books are recommended for reference or further study: in connection with Chapters II and IV, F. Howard Collins, *Author and Printer* (Henry Frowde); Chicago University Press, *Manual of Style;* T. L. De Vinne, *Correct Composition* (The Century Company); Horace Hart, *Rules for Compositors and Printers* (Oxford

University Press); George McLane Wood, *Extracts from the Style-Book of the Government Printing Office* (United States Geological Survey); in connection with Chapters III and V, *The King's English* (Oxford University Press); Sir Arthur Quiller-Couch, *The Art of Writing* (Putnam), especially the chapter, Interlude on Jargon; George McLane Wood, *Suggestions to Authors* (United States Geological Survey); John Lesslie Hall, *English Usage* (Scott, Foresman and Co.); James P. Kelley, *Workmanship in Words* (Little, Brown and Co.). In these will be found full discussions of many points here briefly treated and an abundant store of illustrations to supplement those given in this book.

It is an old observation that the best writers sometimes disregard the rules of rhetoric. When they do so, however, the reader will usually find in the sentence some compensating merit, attained at the cost of the violation. Unless he is certain of doing as well, he will probably do best to follow the rules. After he has learned, by their guidance, to write plain English adequate for everyday uses, let him look, for the secrets of style, to the study of the masters of literature.

II. ELEMENTARY RULES OF USAGE

1. Form the possessive singular of nouns by adding 's.
Follow this rule whatever the final consonant. Thus write,

> Charles's friend
> Burns's poems
> the witch's malice

This is the usage of the United States Government Printing Office and of the Oxford University Press.

Exceptions are the possessive of ancient proper names in *-es* and *-is*, the possessive *Jesus'*, and such forms as *for conscience' sake, for righteousness' sake*. But such forms as *Achilles' heel, Moses' laws, Isis' temple* are commonly replaced by

> the heel of Achilles
> the laws of Moses
> the temple of Isis

The pronominal possessives *hers, its, theirs, yours,* and *oneself* have no apostrophe.

2. In a series of three or more terms with a single conjunction, use a comma after each term except the last.
Thus write,

> red, white, and blue
> gold, silver, or copper
> He opened the letter, read it, and made a note of its contents.

This is also the usage of the Government Printing Office and of the Oxford University Press.

In the names of business firms the last comma is omitted, as,

> Brown, Shipley & Co.

7

3. Enclose parenthetic expressions between commas.

The best way to see a country, unless you are pressed for time, is to travel on foot.

This rule is difficult to apply; it is frequently hard to decide whether a single word, such as *however*, or a brief phrase, is or is not parenthetic. If the interruption to the flow of the sentence is but slight, the writer may safely omit the commas. But whether the interruption be slight or considerable, he must never insert one comma and omit the other. Such punctuation as

Marjorie's husband, Colonel Nelson paid us a visit yesterday,

or

My brother you will be pleased to hear, is now in perfect health,

is indefensible.

If a parenthetic expression is preceded by a conjunction, place the first comma before the conjunction, not after it.

He saw us coming, and unaware that we had learned of his treachery, greeted us with a smile.

Always to be regarded as parenthetic and to be enclosed between commas (or, at the end of the sentence, between comma and period) are the following:

(1) the year, when forming part of a date, and the day of the month, when following the day of the week:

February to July, 1916.
April 6, 1917.
Monday, November 11, 1918.

(2) the abbreviations *etc.* and *jr.*

(3) non-restrictive relative clauses, that is, those which do not serve to identify or define the antecedent noun, and similar clauses introduced by conjunctions indicating time or place.

The audience, which had at first been indifferent, became more and more interested.

In this sentence the clause introduced by *which* does not serve to tell which of several possible audiences is meant; what audience is in question is supposed to be already known. The clause adds, parenthetically, a statement supplementing that in the main clause. The sentence is virtually a combination of two statements which might have been made independently:

The audience had at first been indifferent. It became more and more interested.

Compare the restrictive relative clause, not set off by commas, in the sentence,

The candidate who best meets these requirements will obtain the place.

Here the clause introduced by *who* does serve to tell which of several possible candidates is meant; the sentence cannot be split up into two independent statements.

The difference in punctuation in the two sentences following is based on the same principle:

Nether Stowey, where Coleridge wrote *The Rime of the Ancient Mariner*, is a few miles from Bridgewater.
The day will come when you will admit your mistake.

Nether Stowey is completely identified by its name; the statement about Coleridge is therefore supplementary and parenthetic. The *day* spoken of is identified only by the dependent clause, which is therefore restrictive.

Similar in principle to the enclosing of parenthetic expressions between commas is the setting off by commas of phrases or dependent clauses preceding or following the main clause of a sentence.

Partly by hard fighting, partly by diplomatic skill, they enlarged their dominions to the east, and rose to royal rank with the possession of Sicily, exchanged afterwards for Sardinia.

Other illustrations may be found in sentences quoted under Rules 4, 5, 6, 7, 16, and 18.

The writer should be careful not to set off independent clauses by commas: see under Rule 5.

4. Place a comma before a conjunction introducing a co-ordinate clause.

The early records of the city have disappeared, and the story of its first years can no longer be reconstructed.

The situation is perilous, but there is still one chance of escape.

Sentences of this type, isolated from their context, may seem to be in need of rewriting. As they make complete sense when the comma is reached, the second clause has the appearance of an afterthought. Further, *and* is the least specific of connectives. Used between independent clauses, it indicates only that a relation exists between them without defining that relation. In the example above, the relation is that of cause and result. The two sentences might be rewritten:

As the early records of the city have disappeared, the story of its first years can no longer be reconstructed.

Although the situation is perilous, there is still one chance of escape.

Or the subordinate clauses might be replaced by phrases:

Owing to the disappearance of the early records of the city, the story of its first years can no longer be reconstructed.

In this perilous situation, there is still one chance of escape.

But a writer may err by making his sentences too uniformly compact and periodic, and an occasional loose sentence prevents the style from becoming too formal and gives the reader a certain relief. Consequently, loose sentences of the type first quoted are common in easy, unstudied writing. But a writer should be careful not to construct too many of his sentences after this pattern (see Rule 14).

Two-part sentences of which the second member is introduced by *as* (in the sense of *because*), *for*, *or*, *nor*, and *while* (in the sense of *and at the same time*) likewise require a comma before the conjunction.

If the second member is introduced by an adverb, a semicolon, not a comma, is required (see Rule 5). The connectives *so* and *yet* may be used either as adverbs or as conjunctions, accordingly as the second clause is felt to be co-ordinate or subordinate; consequently either mark of punctuation may be justified. But these uses of *so* (equivalent to *accordingly* or to *so that*) are somewhat colloquial and should, as a rule, be avoided in writing. A simple correction, usually serviceable, is to omit the word *so* and begin the first clause with *as* or *since:*

I had never been in the place before; so I had difficulty in finding my way about.	As I had never been in the place before, I had difficulty in finding my way about.

If a dependent clause, or an introductory phrase requiring to be set off by a comma, precedes the second independent clause, no comma is needed after the conjunction.

The situation is perilous, but if we are prepared to act promptly, there is still one chance of escape.

When the subject is the same for both clauses and is expressed only once, a comma is required if the connective is *but*. If the connective is *and*, the comma should be omitted if the relation between the two statements is close or immediate.

I have heard his arguments, but am still unconvinced.
He has had several years' experience and is thoroughly competent.

5. Do not join independent clauses by a comma.

If two or more clauses, grammatically complete and not joined by a conjunction, are to form a single compound sentence, the proper mark of punctuation is a semicolon.

Stevenson's romances are entertaining; they are full of exciting adventures.
It is nearly half past five; we cannot reach town before dark.

It is of course equally correct to write the above as two sentences each, replacing the semicolons by periods.

11

Stevenson's romances are entertaining. They are full of exciting adventures.

It is nearly half past five. We cannot reach town before dark.

If a conjunction is inserted the proper mark is a comma (Rule 4).

Stevenson's romances are entertaining, for they are full of exciting adventures.

It is nearly half past five, and we cannot reach town before dark.

A comparison of the three forms given above will show clearly the advantage of the first. It is, at least in the examples given, better than the second form, because it suggests the close relationship between the two statements in a way that the second does not attempt, and better than the third, because briefer and therefore more forcible. Indeed it may be said that this simple method of indicating relationship between statements is one of the most useful devices of composition. The relationship, as above, is commonly one of cause or of consequence.

Note that if the second clause is preceded by an adverb, such as *accordingly, besides, then, therefore,* or *thus,* and not by a conjunction, the semicolon is still required.

Two exceptions to the rule may be admitted. If the clauses are very short, and are alike in form, a comma is usually permissible:

Man proposes, God disposes.

The gate swung apart, the bridge fell, the portcullis was drawn up.

Note that in these examples the relation is not one of cause or consequence. Also in the colloquial form of expression,

I hardly knew him, he was so changed,

a comma, not a semicolon, is required. But this form of expression is inappropriate in writing, except in the dialogue of a story or play, or perhaps in a familiar letter.

6. Do not break sentences in two.

In other words, do not use periods for commas.

I met them on a Cunard liner several years ago. Coming home from Liverpool to New York.

He was an interesting talker. A man who had traveled all over the world and lived in half a dozen countries.

In both these examples, the first period should be replaced by a comma, and the following word begun with a small letter.

It is permissible to make an emphatic word or expression serve the purpose of a sentence and to punctuate it accordingly:

> Again and again he called out. No reply.

The writer must, however, be certain that the emphasis is warranted, and that he will not be suspected of a mere blunder in syntax or in punctuation.

Rules 3, 4, 5, and 6 cover the most important principles in the punctuation of ordinary sentences; they should be so thoroughly mastered that their application becomes second nature.

7. A participial phrase at the beginning of a sentence must refer to the grammatical subject.

> Walking slowly down the road, he saw a woman accompanied by two children.

The word *walking* refers to the subject of the sentence, not to the woman. If the writer wishes to make it refer to the woman, he must recast the sentence:

> He saw a woman accompanied by two children, walking slowly down the road.

Participial phrases preceded by a conjunction or by a preposition, nouns in apposition, adjectives, and adjective phrases come under the same rule if they begin the sentence.

On arriving in Chicago, his friends met him at the station.	When he arrived (or, On his arrival) in Chicago, his friends met him at the station.

13

A soldier of proved valor, they entrusted him with the defence of the city.

A soldier of proved valor, he was entrusted with the defence of the city.

Young and inexperienced, the task seemed easy to me.

Young and inexperienced, I thought the task easy.

Without a friend to counsel him, the temptation proved irresistible.

Without a friend to counsel him, he found the temptation irresistible.

Sentences violating this rule are often ludicrous.

Being in a dilapidated condition, I was able to buy the house very cheap.

Wondering irresolutely what to do next, the clock struck twelve.

III. ELEMENTARY PRINCIPLES OF COMPOSITION

8. Make the paragraph the unit of composition: one paragraph to each topic.

If the subject on which you are writing is of slight extent, or if you intend to treat it very briefly, there may be no need of subdividing it into topics. Thus a brief description, a brief summary of a literary work, a brief account of a single incident, a narrative merely outlining an action, the setting forth of a single idea, any one of these is best written in a single paragraph. After the paragraph has been written, examine it to see whether subdivision will not improve it.

Ordinarily, however, a subject requires subdivision into topics, each of which should be made the subject of a paragraph. The object of treating each topic in a paragraph by itself is, of course, to aid the reader. The beginning of each paragraph is a signal to him that a new step in the development of the subject has been reached.

The extent of subdivision will vary with the length of the composition. For example, a short notice of a book or poem might consist of a single paragraph. One slightly longer might consist of two paragraphs:

    A. Account of the work.

    B. Critical discussion.

A report on a poem, written for a class in literature, might consist of seven paragraphs:

    A. Facts of composition and publication.

    B. Kind of poem; metrical form.

    C. Subject.

    D. Treatment of subject.

    E. For what chiefly remarkable.

F. Wherein characteristic of the writer.

G. Relationship to other works.

The contents of paragraphs C and D would vary with the poem. Usually, paragraph C would indicate the actual or imagined circumstances of the poem (the situation), if these call for explanation, and would then state the subject and outline its development. If the poem is a narrative in the third person throughout, paragraph C need contain no more than a concise summary of the action. Paragraph D would indicate the leading ideas and show how they are made prominent, or would indicate what points in the narrative are chiefly emphasized.

A novel might be discussed under the heads:

A. Setting.

B. Plot.

C. Characters.

D. Purpose.

An historical event might be discussed under the heads:

A. What led up to the event.

B. Account of the event.

C. What the event led up to.

In treating either of these last two subjects, the writer would probably find it necessary to subdivide one or more of the topics here given.

As a rule, single sentences should not be written or printed as paragraphs. An exception may be made of sentences of transition, indicating the relation between the parts of an exposition or argument. Frequent exceptions are also necessary in textbooks, guidebooks, and other works in which many topics are treated briefly.

In dialogue, each speech, even if only a single word, is a paragraph by itself; that is, a new paragraph begins with each change of speaker. The application of this rule, when dialogue and narrative are combined, is best learned from examples in well-printed works of fiction.

9. As a rule, begin each paragraph with a topic sentence, end it in conformity with the beginning.

Again, the object is to aid the reader. The practice here recommended enables him to discover the purpose of each paragraph as he begins to read it, and to retain this purpose in mind as he ends it. For this reason, the most generally useful kind of paragraph, particularly in exposition and argument, is that in which

(a) the topic sentence comes at or near the beginning;

(b) the succeeding sentences explain or establish or develop the statement made in the topic sentence; and

(c) the final sentence either emphasizes the thought of the topic sentence or states some important consequence.

Ending with a digression, or with an unimportant detail, is particularly to be avoided.

If the paragraph forms part of a larger composition, its relation to what precedes, or its function as a part of the whole, may need to be expressed. This can sometimes be done by a mere word or phrase (*again; therefore; for the same reason*) in the topic sentence. Sometimes, however, it is expedient to precede the topic sentence by one or more sentences of introduction or transition. If more than one such sentence is required, it is generally better to set apart the transitional sentences as a separate paragraph.

According to the writer's purpose, he may, as indicated above, relate the body of the paragraph to the topic sentence in one or more of several different ways. He may make the meaning of the topic sentence clearer by restating it in other forms, by defining its terms, by denying the contrary, by giving illustrations or specific instances; he may establish it by proofs; or he may develop it by showing its implications and consequences. In a long paragraph, he may carry out several of these processes.

[1]Now, to be properly enjoyed, a walking tour should be gone upon alone. [2]If you go in a company, or even in pairs, it is no longer a walking tour in anything but name; it is something else and more in the

17

nature of a picnic. ³A walking tour should be gone upon alone, because freedom is of the essence; because you should be able to stop and go on, and follow this way or that, as the freak takes you; and because you must have your own pace, and neither trot alongside a champion walker, nor mince in time with a girl. ⁴And you must be open to all impressions and let your thoughts take colour from what you see. ⁵You should be as a pipe for any wind to play upon. ⁶"I cannot see the wit," says Hazlitt, "of walking and talking at the same time. ⁷When I am in the country, I wish to vegetate like the country," which is the gist of all that can be said upon the matter. ⁸There should be no cackle of voices at your elbow, to jar on the meditative silence of the morning. ⁹And so long as a man is reasoning he cannot surrender himself to that fine intoxication that comes of much motion in the open air, that begins in a sort of dazzle and sluggishness of the brain, and ends in a peace that passes comprehension.—Stevenson, *Walking Tours*.

¹Topic sentence. ²The meaning made clearer by denial of the contrary. ³The topic sentence repeated, in abridged form, and supported by three reasons; the meaning of the third ("you must have your own pace") made clearer by denying the contrary. ⁴A fourth reason, stated in two forms. ⁵The same reason, stated in still another form. ⁶⁻⁷The same reason as stated by Hazlitt. ⁸Repetition, in paraphrase, of the quotation from Hazlitt. ⁹Final statement of the fourth reason, in language amplified and heightened to form a strong conclusion.

¹It was chiefly in the eighteenth century that a very different conception of history grew up. ²Historians then came to believe that their task was not so much to paint a picture as to solve a problem; to explain or illustrate the successive phases of national growth, prosperity, and adversity. ³The history of morals, of industry, of intellect, and of art; the changes that take place in manners or beliefs; the dominant ideas that prevailed in successive periods; the rise, fall, and modification of political constitutions; in a word, all the conditions of national well-being became the subject of their works. ⁴They sought rather to write a history of peoples than a history of kings. ⁵They looked especially in history for the chain of causes and effects. ⁶They undertook to study in the past the physiology of nations, and hoped by applying the experimental method on a large scale to deduce some lessons of real value about the conditions on which the welfare of society mainly depend.—Lecky, *The Political Value of History*.

¹Topic sentence. ²The meaning of the topic sentence made clearer; the new conception of history defined. ³The definition expanded. ⁴The definition explained by contrast. ⁵The definition supplemented: another element in the new conception of history. ⁶Conclusion: an important consequence of the new conception of history.

18

In narration and description the paragraph sometimes begins with a concise, comprehensive statement serving to hold together the details that follow.

The breeze served us admirably.
The campaign opened with a series of reverses.
The next ten or twelve pages were filled with a curious set of entries.

But this device, if too often used, would become a mannerism. More commonly the opening sentence simply indicates by its subject with what the paragraph is to be principally concerned.

At length I thought I might return towards the stockade.
He picked up the heavy lamp from the table and began to explore.
Another flight of steps, and they emerged on the roof.

The brief paragraphs of animated narrative, however, are often without even this semblance of a topic sentence. The break between them serves the purpose of a rhetorical pause, throwing into prominence some detail of the action.

10. Use the active voice.

The active voice is usually more direct and vigorous than the passive:

I shall always remember my first visit to Boston.

This is much better than

My first visit to Boston will always be remembered by me.

The latter sentence is less direct, less bold, and less concise. If the writer tries to make it more concise by omitting "by me,"

My first visit to Boston will always be remembered,

it becomes indefinite: is it the writer, or some person undisclosed, or the world at large, that will always remember this visit?

This rule does not, of course, mean that the writer should entirely discard the passive voice, which is frequently convenient and sometimes necessary.

The dramatists of the Restoration are little esteemed to-day.

Modern readers have little esteem for the dramatists of the Restoration.

The first would be the right form in a paragraph on the dramatists of the Restoration; the second, in a paragraph on the tastes of modern readers. The need of making a particular word the subject of the sentence will often, as in these examples, determine which voice is to be used.

As a rule, avoid making one passive depend directly upon another.

Gold was not allowed to be exported.	It was forbidden to export gold (The export of gold was prohibited).
He has been proved to have been seen entering the building.	It has been proved that he was seen to enter the building.

In both the examples above, before correction, the word properly related to the second passive is made the subject of the first.

A common fault is to use as the subject of a passive construction a noun which expresses the entire action, leaving to the verb no function beyond that of completing the sentence.

A survey of this region was made in 1900.	This region was surveyed in 1900.
Mobilization of the army was rapidly effected.	The army was rapidly mobilized.
Confirmation of these reports cannot be obtained.	These reports cannot be confirmed.

Compare the sentence. "The export of gold was prohibited," in which the predicate "was prohibited" expresses something not implied in "export."

The habitual use of the active voice makes for forcible writing. This is true not only in narrative principally concerned with action, but in writing of any kind. Many a tame sentence of description or exposition can be made lively and emphatic by substituting a verb in the active voice for some such perfunctory expression as *there is*, or *could be heard*.

There were a great number of dead leaves lying on the ground.	Dead leaves covered the ground.
The sound of a guitar somewhere in the house could be heard.	Somewhere in the house a guitar hummed sleepily.
The reason that he left college was that his health became impaired.	Failing health compelled him to leave college.
It was not long before he was very sorry that he had said what he had.	He soon repented his words.

11. Put statements in positive form.

Make definite assertions. Avoid tame, colorless, hesitating, non-committal language. Use the word *not* as a means of denial or in antithesis, never as a means of evasion.

He was not very often on time.	He usually came late.
He did not think that studying Latin was much use.	He thought the study of Latin useless.
The Taming of the Shrew is rather weak in spots. Shakespeare does not portray Katharine as a very admirable character, nor does Bianca remain long in memory as an important character in Shakespeare's works.	The women in *The Taming of the Shrew* are unattractive. Katharine is disagreeable, Bianca insignificant.

The last example, before correction, is indefinite as well as negative. The corrected version, consequently, is simply a guess at the writer's intention.

All three examples show the weakness inherent in the word *not*. Consciously or unconsciously, the reader is dissatisfied with being told only what is not; he wishes to be told what is. Hence, as a rule, it is better to express even a negative in positive form.

not honest	dishonest
not important	trifling
did not remember	forgot
did not pay any attention to	ignored
did not have much confidence in	distrusted

The antithesis of negative and positive is strong:

Not charity, but simple justice.
Not that I loved Caesar less, but Rome the more.

Negative words other than *not* are usually strong:

The sun never sets upon the British flag.

12. Use definite, specific, concrete language.

Prefer the specific to the general, the definite to the vague, the concrete to the abstract.

A period of unfavorable weather set in.	It rained every day for a week.
He showed satisfaction as he took possession of his well-earned reward.	He grinned as he pocketed the coin.
There is a general agreement among those who have enjoyed the experience that surf-riding is productive of great exhilaration.	All who have tried surf-riding agree that it is most exhilarating.

If those who have studied the art of writing are in accord on any one point, it is on this, that the surest method of arousing and holding the attention of the reader is by being specific, definite, and concrete. Critics have pointed out how much of the effectiveness of the greatest writers, Homer, Dante, Shakespeare, results from their constant definiteness and concreteness. Browning, to cite a more modern author, affords many striking examples. Take, for instance, the lines from *My Last Duchess*,

> Sir, 'twas all one! My favour at her breast,
> The dropping of the daylight in the west,
> The bough of cherries some officious fool
> Broke in the orchard for her, the white mule
> She rode with round the terrace—all and each
> Would draw from her alike the approving speech,
> Or blush, at least,

and those which end the poem,

> Notice Neptune, though,
> Taming a sea-horse, thought a rarity,
> Which Claus of Innsbruck cast in bronze for me.

These words call up pictures. Recall how in *The Bishop Orders his Tomb in St. Praxed's Church* "the Renaissance spirit—its worldliness, inconsistency, pride, hypocrisy, ignorance of itself, love of art, of luxury, of good Latin," to quote Ruskin's comment on the poem, is made manifest in specific details and in concrete terms.

Prose, in particular narrative and descriptive prose, is made vivid by the same means. If the experiences of Jim Hawkins and of David Balfour, of Kim, of Nostromo, have seemed for the moment real to countless readers, if in reading Carlyle we have almost the sense of being physically present at the taking of the Bastille, it is because of the definiteness of the details and the concreteness of the terms used. It is not that every detail is given; that would be impossible, as well as to no purpose; but that all the significant details are given, and not vaguely, but with such definiteness that the reader, in imagination, can project himself into the scene.

In exposition and in argument, the writer must likewise never lose his hold upon the concrete, and even when he is dealing with general principles, he must give particular instances of their application.

"This superiority of specific expressions is clearly due to the effort required to translate words into thoughts. As we do not think in generals, but in particulars—as whenever any class of things is referred to, we represent it to ourselves by calling to mind individual members of it, it follows that when an abstract word is used, the hearer or reader has to choose, from his stock of images, one or more by which he may figure to himself the genus mentioned. In doing this, some delay must arise, some force be expended; and if by employing a specific term an appropriate image can be at once suggested, an economy is achieved, and a more vivid impression produced."

Herbert Spencer, from whose *Philosophy of Style* the preceding paragraph is quoted, illustrates the principle by the sentences:

23

| In proportion as the manners, customs, and amusements of a nation are cruel and barbarous, the regulations of their penal code will be severe. | In proportion as men delight in battles, bull-fights, and combats of gladiators, will they punish by hanging, burning, and the rack. |

13. Omit needless words.

Vigorous writing is concise. A sentence should contain no unnecessary words, a paragraph no unnecessary sentences, for the same reason that a drawing should have no unnecessary lines and a machine no unnecessary parts. This requires not that the writer make all his sentences short, or that he avoid all detail and treat his subjects only in outline, but that he make every word tell.

Many expressions in common use violate this principle:

the question as to whether	whether (the question whether)
there is no doubt but that	no doubt (doubtless)
used for fuel purposes	used for fuel
he is a man who	he
in a hasty manner	hastily
this is a subject which	this subject
His story is a strange one.	His story is strange.

In especial the expression *the fact that* should be revised out of every sentence in which it occurs.

owing to the fact that	since (because)
in spite of the fact that	though (although)
call your attention to the fact that	remind you (notify you)
I was unaware of the fact that	I was unaware that (did not know)
the fact that he had not succeeded	his failure
the fact that I had arrived	my arrival

See also under *case, character, nature, system* in Chapter V. *Who is, which was,* and the like are often superfluous.

His brother, who is a member of the same firm	His brother, a member of the same firm
Trafalgar, which was Nelson's last battle	Trafalgar, Nelson's last battle

As positive statement is more concise than negative, and the active voice more concise than the passive, many of the examples given under Rules 11 and 12 illustrate this rule as well.

A common violation of conciseness is the presentation of a single complex idea, step by step, in a series of sentences or independent clauses which might to advantage be combined into one.

Macbeth was very ambitious. This led him to wish to become king of Scotland. The witches told him that this wish of his would come true. The king of Scotland at this time was Duncan. Encouraged by his wife, Macbeth murdered Duncan. He was thus enabled to succeed Duncan as king. (51 words.)	Encouraged by his wife, Macbeth achieved his ambition and realized the prediction of the witches by murdering Duncan and becoming king of Scotland in his place. (26 words.)
There were several less important courses, but these were the most important, and although they did not come every day, they came often enough to keep you in such a state of mind that you never knew what your next move would be. (43 words.)	These, the most important courses of all, came, if not daily, at least often enough to keep one under constant strain. (21 words.)

14. Avoid a succession of loose sentences:

This rule refers especially to loose sentences of a particular type, those consisting of two co-ordinate clauses, the second introduced by a conjunction or relative   Although single sentences of this type may be unexceptionable (see under Rule 4), a series soon becomes monotonous and tedious.

An unskilful writer will sometimes construct a whole paragraph of sentences of this kind, using as connectives *and, but, so,* and less frequently, *who, which, when, where,* and *while,* these last in non-restrictive senses (see under Rule 3).

The third concert of the subscription series was given last evening, and a large audience was in attendance. Mr. Edward Appleton was the soloist, and the Boston Symphony Orchestra furnished the instrumental music. The former showed himself to be an artist of the first rank, while the latter proved itself fully deserving of its high reputation. The interest aroused by the series has been very gratifying to the Committee, and it is planned to give a similar series annually hereafter. The fourth concert will be given on Tuesday, May 10, when an equally attractive programme will be presented.

Apart from its triteness and emptiness, the paragraph above is weak because of the structure of its sentences, with their mechanical symmetry and sing-song. Contrast with them the sentences in the paragraphs quoted under Rule 9, or in any piece of good English prose, as the preface (Before the Curtain) to *Vanity Fair*.

If the writer finds that he has written a series of sentences of the type described, he should recast enough of them to remove the monotony, replacing them by simple sentences, by sentences of two clauses joined by a semicolon, by periodic sentences of two clauses, by sentences, loose or periodic, of three clauses—whichever best represent the real relations of the thought.

15. Express co-ordinate ideas in similar form.

This principle, that of parallel construction, requires that expressions of similar content and function should be outwardly similar. The likeness of form enables the reader to recognize more readily the likeness of content and function. Familiar instances from the Bible are the Ten Commandments, the Beatitudes, and the petitions of the Lord's Prayer.

The unskillful writer often violates this principle, from a mistaken belief that he should constantly vary the form of his expressions. It is true that in repeating a statement in order to emphasize it he may have need to vary its form. For illustration, see the paragraph from Stevenson quoted under Rule 10. But apart from this, he should follow the principle of parallel construction.

Formerly, science was taught by the textbook method, while now the laboratory method is employed.	Formerly, science was taught by the textbook method; now it is taught by the laboratory method.

The left-hand version gives the impression that the writer is undecided or timid; he seems unable or afraid to choose one form of expression and hold to it. The right-hand version shows that the writer has at least made his choice and abided by it.

By this principle, an article or a preposition applying to all the members of a series must either be used only before the first term or else be repeated before each term.

The French, the Italians, Spanish, and Portuguese	The French, the Italians, the Spanish, and the Portuguese
In spring, summer, or in winter	In spring, summer, or winter (In spring, in summer, or in winter)

Correlative expressions (*both, and; not, but; not only, but also; either, or; first, second, third;* and the like) should be followed by the same grammatical construction, that is, virtually, by the same part of speech. (Such combinations as "both Henry and I," "not silk, but a cheap substitute," are obviously within the rule.) Many violations of this rule (as the first three below) arise from faulty arrangement; others (as the last) from the use of unlike constructions.

It was both a long ceremony and very tedious.	The ceremony was both long and tedious.
A time not for words, but action.	A time not for words, but for action.
Either you must grant his request or incur his ill will.	You must either grant his request or incur his ill will.
My objections are, first, the injustice of the measure; second, that it is unconstitutional.	My objections are, first, that the measure is unjust; second, that it is unconstitutional.

See also the third example under Rule 12 and the last under Rule 13.

It may be asked, what if a writer needs to express a very large number of similar ideas, say twenty? Must he write twenty consecutive sentences of the same pattern? On closer examination he will probably find that the difficulty is imaginary, that his twenty ideas can be classified in groups, and that he need apply the principle only within each group. Otherwise he had best avoid difficulty by putting his statements in the form of a table.

16. Keep related words together.

The position of the words in a sentence is the principal means of showing their relationship. The writer must therefore, so far as possible, bring together the words, and groups of words, that are related in thought, and keep apart those which are not so related.

The subject of a sentence and the principal verb should not, as a rule, be separated by a phrase or clause that can be transferred to the beginning.

Wordsworth, in the fifth book of *The Excursion*, gives a minute description of this church.	In the fifth book of *The Excursion*, Wordsworth gives a minute description of this church.
Cast iron, when treated in a Bessemer converter, is changed into steel.	By treatment in a Bessemer converter, cast iron is changed into steel.

The objection is that the interposed phrase or clause needlessly interrupts the natural order of the main clause. Usually, however, this objection does not hold when the order is interrupted only by a relative clause or by an expression in apposition. Nor does it hold in periodic sentences in which the interruption is a deliberately used means of creating suspense (see examples under Rule 18).

The relative pronoun should come, as a rule, immediately after its antecedent.

There was a look in his eye that boded mischief.	In his eye was a look that boded mischief.
He wrote three articles about his adventures in Spain, which were published in *Harper's Magazine*.	He published in *Harper's Magazine* three articles about his adventures in Spain.

| This is a portrait of Benjamin Harrison, grandson of William Henry Harrison, who became President in 1889. | This is a portrait of Benjamin Harrison, grandson of William Henry Harrison. He became President in 1889. |

If the antecedent consists of a group of words, the relative comes at the end of the group, unless this would cause ambiguity.

The Superintendent of the Chicago Division, who

A proposal to amend the Sherman Act, which has been variously judged.	A proposal, which has been variously judged, to amend the Sherman Act.
	A proposal to amend the much-debated Sherman Act.
The grandson of William Henry Harrison, who	W i l l i a m Henry Harrison's grandson, who

A noun in apposition may come between antecedent and relative, because in such a combination no real ambiguity can arise.

The Duke of York, his brother, who was regarded with hostility by the Whigs

Modifiers should come, if possible, next to the word they modify. If several expressions modify the same word, they should be so arranged that no wrong relation is suggested.

All the members were not present.	Not all the members were present.
He only found two mistakes.	He found only two mistakes.
Major R. E. Joyce will give a lecture on Tuesday evening in Bailey Hall, to which the public is invited, on "My Experiences in Mesopotamia" at eight P. M.	On Tuesday evening at eight P. M., Major R. E. Joyce will give in Bailey Hall a lecture on "My Experiences in Mesopotamia." The public is invited.

17. In summaries, keep to one tense.

In summarizing the action of a drama, the writer should always use the present tense. In summarizing a poem, story, or novel, he should preferably use the present, though he may use the past if he prefers. If the summary is in the present tense, antecedent action should be expressed by the perfect; if in the past, by the past perfect.

An unforeseen chance prevents Friar John from delivering Friar Lawrence's letter to Romeo. Meanwhile, owing to her father's arbitrary change of the day set for her wedding, Juliet has been compelled to drink the potion on Tuesday night, with the result that Balthasar informs Romeo of her supposed death before Friar Lawrence learns of the non-delivery of the letter.

But whichever tense be used in the summary, a past tense in indirect discourse or in indirect question remains unchanged.

The Friar confesses that it was he who married them.

Apart from the exceptions noted, whichever tense the writer chooses, he should use throughout. Shifting from one tense to the other gives the appearance of uncertainty and irresolution (compare Rule 15).

In presenting the statements or the thought of some one else, as in summarizing an essay or reporting a speech, the writer should avoid intercalating such expressions as "he said," "he stated," "the speaker added," "the speaker then went on to say," "the author also thinks," or the like. He should indicate clearly at the outset, once for all, that what follows is summary, and then waste no words in repeating the notification.

In notebooks, in newspapers, in handbooks of literature, summaries of one kind or another may be indispensable, and for children in primary schools it is a useful exercise to retell a story in their own words. But in the criticism or interpretation of literature the writer should be careful to avoid dropping into summary. He may find it necessary to devote one or two sentences to indicating the subject, or the opening situation, of the work he is discussing; he may cite numerous details to illustrate its qualities. But he should aim to write an orderly discussion supported by evidence, not a summary with occasional comment.

Similarly, if the scope of his discussion includes a number of works, he will as a rule do better not to take them up singly in chronological order, but to aim from the beginning at establishing general conclusions.

18. Place the emphatic words of a sentence at the end.

The proper place in the sentence for the word, or group of words, which the writer desires to make most prominent is usually the end.

Humanity has hardly advanced in fortitude since that time, though it has advanced in many other ways.	Humanity, since that time, has advanced in many other ways, but it has hardly advanced in fortitude.
This steel is principally used for making razors, because of its hardness.	Because of its hardness, this steel is principally used in making razors.

The word or group of words entitled to this position of prominence is usually the logical predicate, that is, the *new* element in the sentence, as it is in the second example.

The effectiveness of the periodic sentence arises from the prominence which it gives to the main statement.

Four centuries ago, Christopher Columbus, one of the Italian mariners whom the decline of their own republics had put at the service of the world and of adventure, seeking for Spain a westward passage to the Indies as a set-off against the achievements of Portuguese discoverers, lighted on America.

With these hopes and in this belief I would urge you, laying aside all hindrance, thrusting away all private aims, to devote yourself unswervingly and unflinchingly to the vigorous and successful prosecution of this war.

The other prominent position in the sentence is the beginning. Any element in the sentence, other than the subject, may become emphatic when placed first.

Deceit or treachery he could never forgive.

So vast and rude, fretted by the action of nearly three thousand years, the fragments of this architecture may often seem, at first sight, like works of nature.

31

A subject coming first in its sentence may be emphatic, but hardly by its position alone.   In the sentence,

Great kings worshipped at his shrine,

the emphasis upon *kings* arises largely from its meaning and from the context.   To receive special emphasis, the subject of a sentence must take the position of the predicate.

Through the middle of the valley flowed a winding stream.

The principle that the proper place for what is to be made most prominent is the end applies equally to the words of a sentence, to the sentences of a paragraph, and to the paragraphs of a composition.

IV. A FEW MATTERS OF FORM

Headings. Leave a blank line, or its equivalent in space, after the title or heading of a manuscript. On succeeding pages, if using ruled paper, begin on the first line.

Numerals. Do not spell out dates or other serial numbers. Write them in figures or in Roman notation, as may be appropriate.

August 9, 1918 (9 August 1918)   Chapter XII
Rule 3   352nd Infantry

Parentheses. A sentence containing an expression in parenthesis is punctuated, outside of the marks of parenthesis, exactly as if the expression in parenthesis were absent. The expression within is punctuated as if it stood by itself, except that the final stop is omitted unless it is a question mark or an exclamation point.

I went to his house yesterday (my third attempt to see him), but he had left town.

He declares (and why should we doubt his good faith?) that he is now certain of success.

(When a wholly detached expression or sentence is parenthesized, the final stop comes before the last mark of parenthesis.)

Quotations. Formal quotations, cited as documentary evidence, are introduced by a colon and enclosed in quotation marks.

The provision of the Constitution is: ''No tax or duty shall be laid on articles exported from any state.''

Quotations grammatically in apposition or the direct objects of verbs are preceded by a comma and enclosed in quotation marks.

I recall the maxim of La Rochefoucauld, "Gratitude is a lively sense of benefits to come."

Aristotle says, "Art is an imitation of nature."

Quotations of an entire line, or more, of verse, are begun on a fresh line and centered, but need not be enclosed in quotation marks.

Wordsworth's enthusiasm for the Revolution was at first unbounded:

> Bliss was it in that dawn to be alive,
> But to be young was very heaven!

Quotations introduced by *that* are regarded as in indirect discourse and not enclosed in quotation marks.

Keats declares that beauty is truth, truth beauty.

Proverbial expressions and familiar phrases of literary origin require no quotation marks.

These are the times that try men's souls.
He lives far from the madding crowd.

The same is true of colloquialisms and slang.

References. In scholarly work requiring exact references, abbreviate titles that occur frequently, giving the full forms in an alphabetical list at the end. As a general practice, give the references in parenthesis or in footnotes, not in the body of the sentence. Omit the words *act, scene, line, book, volume, page*, except when referring by only one of them. Punctuate as indicated below.

In the second scene of the third act	In iii.ii (still better, simply insert iii.ii in parenthesis at the proper place in the sentence)

After the killing of Polonius, Hamlet is placed under guard (iv.ii. 14).

2 *Samuel* i:17–27

Othello ii.iii. 264–267, iii.iii. 155–161.

Syllabication. If there is room at the end of a line for one or more syllables of a word, but not for the whole word, divide the word, unless this involves cutting off only a single letter, or cutting off only two letters of a long word. No hard and fast rule for all words can be laid down. The principles most frequently applicable are:

(a) Divide the word according to its formation:

know-ledge (not knowl-edge); Shake-speare (not Shakes-peare); de-scribe (not des-cribe); atmo-sphere (not atmos-phere);

(b) Divide "on the vowel:"

edi-ble (not ed-ible); propo-sition; ordi-nary; espe-cial; reli-gious; oppo-nents; regu-lar; classi-fi-ca-tion (three divisions allowable); deco-rative; presi-dent;

(c) Divide between double letters, unless they come at the end of the simple form of the word:

Apen-nines; Cincin-nati; refer-ring; but tell-ing.

(d) Do not divide before final -ed if the e is silent:

treat-ed (but not roam-ed or nam-ed).

The treatment of consonants in combination is best shown from examples:

for-tune; pic-ture; sin-gle; presump-tuous; illus-tration; sub-stan-tial (either division); indus-try; instruc-tion; sug-ges-tion; incen-diary.

The student will do well to examine the syllable-division in a number of pages of any carefully printed book.

Titles. For the titles of literary works, scholarly usage prefers italics with capitalized initials. The usage of editors and publishers varies, some using italics with capitalized initials, others using Roman with capitalized initials and with or without quotation marks. Use italics (indicated in manuscript by underscoring), except in writing for a periodical that follows a different practice. Omit initial *A* or *The* from titles when you place the possessive before them.

The *Iliad;* the *Odyssey; As You Like It; To a Skylark; The New-comes; A Tale of Two Cities;* Dickens's *Tale of Two Cities.*

V. WORDS AND EXPRESSIONS COMMONLY MISUSED

(Some of the forms here listed, as *like I did*, are downright bad English; others, as the split infinitive, have their defenders, but are in such general disfavor that it is at least inadvisable to use them; still others, as *case, factor, feature, interesting, one of the most*, are good in their place, but are constantly obtruding themselves into places where they have no right to be. If the writer will make it his purpose from the beginning to express accurately his own individual thought, and will refuse to be satisfied with a ready-made formula that saves him the trouble of doing so, this last set of expressions will cause him little trouble. But if he finds that in a moment of inadvertence he has used one of them, his proper course will probably be not to patch up the sentence by substituting one word or set of words for another, but to recast it completely, as illustrated in a number of examples below and in others under Rules 12 and 13.)

All right. Idiomatic in familiar speech as a detached phrase in the sense, "Agreed," or "Go ahead." In other uses better avoided. Always written as two words.

As good or better than. Expressions of this type should be corrected by rearranging the sentence.

My opinion is as good or better than his.	My opinion is as good as his, or better (if not better).

As to whether. *Whether* is sufficient; see under Rule 13.

Bid. Takes the infinitive without *to*. The past tense in the sense, "ordered") is *bade*.

But. Unnecessary after *doubt* and *help*.

I have no doubt but that	I have no doubt that
He could not help see but that	He could not help seeing that

36

The too frequent use of *but* as a conjunction leads to the fault discussed under Rule 14. A loose sentence formed with *but* can always be converted into a periodic sentence formed with *although*, as illustrated under Rule 4.

Particularly awkward is the following of one *but* by another, making a contrast to a contrast or a reservation to a reservation. This is easily corrected by re-arrangement.

America had vast resources, but she seemed almost wholly unprepared for war. But within a year she had created an army of four million men.	America seemed almost wholly unprepared for war, but she had vast resources. Within a year she had created an army of four million men.

Can. Means *am* (*is, are*) *able*. Not to be used as a substitute for *may*.

Case. The *Concise Oxford Dictionary* begins its definition of this word: "instance of a thing's occurring; usual state of affairs." In these two senses, the word is usually unnecessary.

In many cases, the rooms were poorly ventilated.	Many of the rooms were poorly ventilated.
It has rarely been the case that any mistake has been made.	Few mistakes have been made.

See Wood, *Suggestions to Authors*, pp. 68–71, and Quiller-Couch, *The Art of Writing*, pp. 103–106.

Certainly. Used indiscriminately by some writers, much as others use *very*, to intensify any and every statement. A mannerism of this kind, bad in speech, is even worse in writing.

Character. Often simply redundant, used from a mere habit of wordiness.

Acts of a hostile character	Hostile acts

Claim, vb. With object-noun, means *lay claim to*. May be used with a dependent clause if this sense is clearly involved: "He claimed that he was the sole surviving heir." (But even here, "claimed to be" would be better.) Not to be used as a substitute for *declare, maintain,* or *charge.*

Clever. This word has been greatly overused; it is best restricted to ingenuity displayed in small matters.

Compare. To *compare to* is to point out or imply resemblances, between objects regarded as essentially of different order; to *compare with* is mainly to point out differences, between objects regarded as essentially of the same order. Thus life has been compared to a pilgrimage, to a drama, to a battle; Congress may be compared with the British Parliament. Paris has been compared to ancient Athens; it may be compared with modern London.

Consider. Not followed by *as* when it means "believe to be." "I consider him thoroughly competent." Compare, " The lecturer considered Cromwell first as soldier and second as administrator," where "considered" means "examined" or "discussed."

Data. A plural, like *phenomena* and *strata.*

These data were tabulated.

Dependable. A needless substitute for *reliable, trustworthy.*

Different than. Not permissible. Substitute *different from, other than,* or *unlike.*

Divided into. Not to be misused for *composed of.* The line is sometimes difficult to draw; doubtless plays are divided into acts, but poems are composed of stanzas.

Don't. Contraction of *do not.* The contraction of *does not* is *doesn't.*

Due to. Incorrectly used for *through, because of,* or *owing to,* in adverbial phrases: "He lost the first game, due to carelessness." In correct use related as predicate or as modifier to a particular noun: "This invention is due to Edison;" "losses due to preventable fires."

Folk. A collective noun, equivalent to *people.* Use the singular form only.

38

Effect. As noun, means *result;* as verb, means to *bring about, accomplish* (not to be confused with *affect*, which means "to influence").

As noun, often loosely used in perfunctory writing about fashions, music, painting, and other arts: "an Oriental effect;" "effects in pale green;" "very delicate effects;" "broad effects;" "subtle effects;" "a charming effect was produced by." The writer who has a definite meaning to express will not take refuge in such vagueness.

Etc. Equivalent to *and the rest, and so forth,* and hence not to be used if one of these would be insufficient, that is, if the reader would be left in doubt as to any important particulars. Least open to objection when it represents the last terms of a list already given in full, or immaterial words at the end of a quotation.

At the end of a list introduced by *such as, for example,* or any similar expression, *etc.* is incorrect.

Fact. Use this word only of matters of a kind capable of direct verification, not of matters of judgment. That a particular event happened on a given date, that lead melts at a certain temperature, are facts. But such conclusions as that Napoleon was the greatest of modern generals, or that the climate of California is delightful, however incontestable they ma ybe, are not properly facts.

On the formula *the fact that,* see under Rule 13.

Factor. A hackneyed word; the expressions of which it forms part can usually be replaced by something more direct and idiomatic.

His superior training was the great factor in his winning the match.	He won the match by being better trained.
Heavy artillery has become an increasingly important factor in deciding battles.	Heavy artillery has played a constantly larger part in deciding battles.

Feature. Another hackneyed word; like *factor* it usually adds nothing to the sentence in which it occurs.

A feature of the entertainment especially worthy of mention was the singing of Miss A.	(Better use the same number of words to tell what Miss A. sang, or if the programme has already been given, to tell how she sang.)

As a verb, in the advertising sense of *offer as a special attraction,* to be avoided.

Fix. Colloquial in America for *arrange, prepare, mend.* In writing restrict it to its literary senses, *fasten, make firm or immovable,* etc.

Get. The colloquial *have got* for *have* should not be used in writing. The preferable form of the participle is *got.*

He is a man who. A common type of redundant expression; see Rule 13.

He is a man who is very ambitious.	He is very ambitious.
Spain is a country which I have always wanted to visit.	I have always wanted to visit Spain.

Help. See under **But.**

However. In the meaning *nevertheless,* not to come first in its sentence or clause.

The roads were almost impassable. However, we at last succeeded in reaching camp.	The roads were almost impassable. At last, however, we succeeded in reaching camp.

When *however* comes first, it means *in whatever way* or *to whatever extent.*

However you advise him, he will probably do as he thinks best.
However discouraging the prospect, he never lost heart.

Interesting. Avoid this word as a perfunctory means of introduction. Instead of announcing that what you are about to tell is interesting, make it so.

An interesting story is told of	(Tell the story without preamble.)
In connection with the anticipated visit of Mr. B. to America, it is interesting to recall that he	Mr. B., who it is expected will soon visit America

Kind of. Not to be used as a substitute for *rather* (before adjectives and verbs), or except in familiar style, for *something like* (before nouns). Restrict it to its literal sense: "Amber is a kind of fossil resin;" "I dislike that kind of notoriety." The same holds true of *sort of*.

Less. Should not be misused for *fewer*.

He had less men than in the previous campaign	He had fewer men than in the previous campaign

Less refers to quantity, *fewer* to number. "His troubles are less than mine" means "His troubles are not so great as mine." "His troubles are fewer than mine" means "His troubles are not so numerous as mine." It is, however, correct to say, "The signers of the petition were less than a hundred," where the round number *a hundred* is something like a collective noun, and *less* is thought of as meaning a less quantity or amount.

Like. Not to be misused for *as*. *Like* governs nouns and pronouns; before phrases and clauses the equivalent word is *as*.

We spent the evening like in the old days.	We spent the evening as in the old days.
He thought like I did.	He thought as I did (like me).

Line, along these lines. *Line* in the sense of *course of procedure, conduct, thought*, is allowable, but has been so much overworked, particularly in the phrase *along these lines*, that a writer who aims at freshness or originality had better discard it entirely.

Mr. B. also spoke along the same lines.	Mr. B. also spoke, to the same effect.
He is studying along the line of French literature.	He is studying French literature.

Literal, literally. Often incorrectly used in support of exaggeration or violent metaphor.

A literal flood of abuse.	A flood of abuse.
Literally dead with fatigue	Almost dead with fatigue (dead tired)

41

Lose out. Meant to be more emphatic than *lose*, but actually less so, because of its commonness. The same holds true of *try out, win out, sign up, register up.* With a number of verbs, *out* and *up* form idiomatic combinations: *find out, run out, turn out, cheer up, dry up, make up,* and others, each distinguishable in meaning from the simple verb. *Lose out* is not.

Most. Not to be used for *almost.*

Most everybody	Almost everybody
Most all the time	Almost all the time

Nature. Often simply redundant, used like *character.*

Acts of a hostile nature.	Hostile acts

Often vaguely used in such expressions as a "lover of nature;" "poems about nature." Unless more specific statements follow, the reader cannot tell whether the poems have to do with natural scenery, rural life, the sunset, the untracked wilderness, or the habits of squirrels.

Near by. Adverbial phrase, not yet fully accepted as good English, though the analogy of *close by* and *hard by* seems to justify it. *Near,* or *near at hand,* is as good, if not better.

Not to be used as an adjective; use *neighboring.*

Oftentimes, ofttimes. Archaic forms, no longer in good use. The modern word is *often.*

One hundred and one. Retain the *and* in this and similar expressions, in accordance with the unvarying usage of English prose from Old English times.

One of the most. Avoid beginning essays or paragraphs with this formula, as, "One of the most interesting developments of modern science is, etc.;" "Switzerland is one of the most interesting countries of Europe." There is nothing wrong in this; it is simply threadbare and forcible-feeble.

A common blunder is to use a singular verb in a relative clause following this or a similar expression, when the relative is the subject.

| One of the ablest men that has attacked this problem. | One of the ablest men that have attacked this problem. |

Participle for verbal noun.

| Do you mind me asking a question? | Do you mind my asking a question? |
| There was little prospect of the Senate accepting even this compromise. | There was little prospect of the Senate's accepting even this compromise. |

In the left-hand column, *asking* and *accepting* are present participles; in the right-hand column, they are verbal nouns (gerunds). The construction shown in the left-hand column is occasionally found, and has its defenders. Yet it is easy to see that the second sentence has to do not with a prospect of the Senate, but with a prospect of accepting. In this example, at least, the construction is plainly illogical.

As the authors of *The King's English* point out, there are sentences apparently, but not really, of this type, in which the possessive is not called for.

I cannot imagine Lincoln refusing his assent to this measure.

In this sentence, what the writer cannot imagine is Lincoln himself, in the act of refusing his assent. Yet the meaning would be virtually the same, except for a slight loss of vividness, if he had written,

I cannot imagine Lincoln's refusing his assent to this measure.

By using the possessive, the writer will always be on the safe side.

In the examples above, the subject of the action is a single, unmodified term, immediately preceding the verbal noun, and the construction is as good as any that could be used. But in any sentence in which it is a mere clumsy substitute for something simpler, or in which the use of the possessive is awkward or impossible, should of course be recast.

| In the event of a reconsideration of the whole matter's becoming necessary | If it should become necessary to reconsider the whole matter |

There was great dissatisfaction with the decision of the arbitrators being favorable to the company.	There was great dissatisfaction that the arbitrators should have decided in favor of the company.

People. *The people* is a political term, not to be confused with *the public*. From the people comes political support or opposition; from the public comes artistic appreciation or commercial patronage.

Phase. Means a stage of transition or development: "the phases of the moon;" "the last phase." Not to be used for *aspect* or *topic*.

Another phase of the subject	Another point (another question)

Possess. Not to be used as a mere substitute for *have* or *own*.

He possessed great courage.	He had great courage (was very brave).
He was the fortunate possessor of	He owned

Prove. The past participle is *proved*.

Respective, respectively. These words may usually be omitted with advantage.

Works of fiction are listed under the names of their respective authors.	Works of fiction are listed under the names of their authors.
The one mile and two mile runs were won by Jones and Cummings respectively.	The one mile and two mile runs were won by Jones and by Cummings.

In some kinds of formal writing, as geometrical proofs, it may be necessary to use *respectively*, but it should not appear in writing on ordinary subjects.

Shall, Will. The future tense requires *shall* for the first person, *will* for the second and third. The formula to express the speaker's belief regarding his future action or state is *I shall*; *I will* expresses his determination or his consent.

Should. See under **Would.**

44

So. Avoid, in writing, the use of *so* as an intensifier: "so good;" "so warm;" "so delightful."

On the use of *so* to introduce clauses, see Rule 4.

Sort of. See under **Kind of.**

Split Infinitive. There is precedent from the fourteenth century downward for interposing an adverb between *to* and the infinitive which it governs, but the construction is in disfavor and is avoided by nearly all careful writers.

To diligently inquire	To inquire diligently

State. Not to be used as a mere substitute for *say, remark.* Restrict it to the sense of *express fully or clearly,* as, "He refused to state his objections."

Student Body. A needless and awkward expression meaning no more than the simple word *students.*

A member of the student body	A student
Popular with the student body	Liked by the students
The student body passed resolutions.	The students passed resolutions.

System. Frequently used without need.

Dayton has adopted the commission system of government	Dayton has adopted government by commission.
The dormitory system	Dormitories

Thanking You in Advance. This sounds as if the writer meant, "It will not be worth my while to write to you again." In making your request, write, "Will you please," or "I shall be obliged," and if anything further seems necessary write a letter of acknowledgment later.

They. A common inaccuracy is the use of the plural pronoun when the antecedent is a distributive expression such as *each, each one, everybody, every one, many a man,* which, though implying more than one person, requires the pronoun to be in the singular. Similar to this, but with even less justification, is the use of the plural pronoun with the antecedent *anybody, any one, somebody, some one,* the intention being either to avoid the awkward "he or she,"

45

or to avoid committing oneself to either. Some bashful speakers even say, "A friend of mine told me that they, etc."

Use *he* with all the above words, unless the antecedent is or must be feminine.

Very. Use this word sparingly. Where emphasis is necessary, use words strong in themselves.

Viewpoint. Write *point of view*, but do not misuse this, as many do, for *view* or *opinion*.

While. Avoid the indiscriminate use of this word for *and, but,* and *although.* Many writers use it frequently as a substitute for *and* or *but*, either from a mere desire to vary the connective, or from uncertainty which of the two connectives is the more appropriate. In this use it is best replaced by a semicolon.

The office and salesrooms are on the ground floor, while the rest of the building is devoted to manufacturing.	The office and salesrooms are on the ground floor; the rest of the building is devoted to manufacturing.

Its use as a virtual equivalent of *although* is allowable in sentences where this leads to no ambiguity or absurdity.

While I admire his energy, I wish it were employed in a better cause.

This is entirely correct, as shown by the paraphrase,

I admire his energy; at the same time I wish it were employed in a better cause.

Compare:

While the temperature reaches 90 or 95 degrees in the daytime, the nights are often chilly.	Although the temperature reaches 90 or 95 degrees in the daytime, the nights are often chilly.

The paraphrase,

The temperature reaches 90 or 95 degrees in the daytime; at the same time the nights are often chilly, shows why the use of *while* is incorrect.

In general, the writer will do well to use *while* only with strict literalness, in the sense of *during the time that*.

Whom. Often incorrectly used for *who* before *he said* or similar expressions, when it is really the subject of a following verb.

His brother, whom he said would send him the money	His brother, who he said would send him the money
The man whom he thought was his friend	The man who (that) he thought was his friend (whom he thought his friend)

Worth while. Overworked as a term of vague approval and (with *not*) of disapproval. Strictly applicable only to actions: "Is it worth while to telegraph?"

His books are not worth while.	His books are not worth reading (are not worth one's while to read; do not repay reading; are worthless).

The use of *worth while* before a noun ("a worth while story") is indefensible.

Would. A conditional statement in the first person requires *should*, not *would*.

I should not have succeeded without his help.

The equivalent of *shall* in indirect quotation after a verb in the past tense is *should*, not *would*.

He predicted that before long we should have a great surprise.

To express habitual or repeated action, the past tense, without *would*, is usually sufficient, and from its brevity, more emphatic.

Once a year he would visit the old mansion.	Once a year he visited the old mansion.

47

VI. SPELLING

The spelling of English words is not fixed and invariable, nor does it depend on any other authority than general agreement. At the present day there is practically unanimous agreement as to the spelling of most words. In the list below, for example, *rime* for *rhyme* is the only allowable variation; all the other forms are co-extensive with the English language. At any given moment, however, a relatively small number of words may be spelled in more than one way. Gradually, as a rule, one of these forms comes to be generally preferred, and the less customary form comes to look obsolete and is discarded. From time to time new forms, mostly simplifications, are introduced by innovators, and either win their place or die of neglect.

The practical objection to unaccepted and over-simplified spellings is the disfavor with which they are received by the reader. They distract his attention and exhaust his patience. He reads the form *though* automatically, without thought of its needless complexity; he reads the abbreviation *tho* and mentally supplies the missing letters, at the cost of a fraction of his attention. The writer has defeated his own purpose.

WORDS OFTEN MISSPELLED

accidentally	criticize	duel
advice	deceive	ecstasy
affect	definite	effect
believe	describe	embarass
benefit	despise	existence
challenge	develop	fascinate
coarse	disappoint	fiery
course	dissipate	formerly

48

humorous
hypocrisy
immediately
impostor
incident
incidentally
latter
led
lose
marriage
mischief
murmur
necessary
occurred

opportunity
parallel
Philip
playwright
preceding
prejudice
principal
principle
privilege
pursue
repetition
rhyme
rhythm
ridiculous

sacrilegious
seize
separate
shepherd
siege
similar
simile
too
tragedy
tries
undoubtedly
until
villain

Note that a single consonant (other than *v*) preceded by a stressed short vowel is doubled before *-ed* and *-ing*: *planned, letting, beginning*. (*Coming* is an exception.)

Write *to-day, to-night, to-morrow* (but not *together*) with a hyphen.

Write *any one, every one, some one, some time* (except in the sense of *formerly*) as two words.

VII. EXERCISES ON CHAPTERS II AND III

I. Punctuate:

1. In 1788 the King's advisers warned him that the nation was facing bankruptcy therefore he summoned a body called the States-General believing that it would authorize him to levy new taxes. The people of France however were suffering from burdensome taxation oppressive social injustice and acute scarcity of food and their representatives refused to consider projects of taxation until social and economic reforms should be granted. The King who did not realize the gravity of the situation tried to overawe them collecting soldiers in and about Versailles where the sessions were being held. The people of Paris seeing the danger organized militia companies to defend their representatives. In order to supply themselves with arms they attacked the Invalides and the Bastille which contained the principal supplies of arms and munitions in Paris.

2. On his first continental tour begun in 1809 Byron visited Portugal Spain Albania Greece and Turkey. Of this tour he composed a poetical journal Childe Harold's Pilgrimage in which he ascribed his experiences and reflections not to himself but to a fictitious character Childe Harold described as a melancholy young nobleman prematurely familiar with evil sated with pleasures and embittered against humanity. The substantial merits of the work however lay not in this shadowy and somewhat theatrical figure but in Byron's spirited descriptions of wild or picturesque scenes and in his eloquent championing of Spain and Greece against their oppressors. On his return to England in 1811 he was persuaded rather against his own judgment into allowing the work to be published. Its success was almost unprecedented in his own words he awoke and found himself famous.

II. Explain the difference in meaning:

3. 'God save thee, ancyent Marinere!
'From the fiends that plague thee thus—
        Lyrical Ballads, 1798.
'God save thee, ancient Mariner!
From the fiends, that plague thee thus!—
        Lyrical Ballads, 1800.

III. Explain and correct the errors in punctuation:

4. This course is intended for Freshmen, who in the opinion of the Department are not qualified for military drill.

5. A restaurant, not a cafeteria where good meals are served at popular prices.—*Advt.*

6. The poets of *The Nation,* for all their intensity of patriotic feeling, followed the English rather than the Celtic tradition, their work has a political rather than a literary value and bears little upon the development of modern Irish verse.

7. We were in one of the strangest places imaginable. A long and narrow passage overhung on either side by a stupendous barrier of black and threatening rocks.

8. Only a few years ago after a snow storm in the passes not far north of Jerusalem no less than twenty-six Russian pilgrims perished amidst the snow. One cannot help thinking largely because they made little attempt to save themselves.

IV. Point out and correct the faults in the following sentences:

9. During childhood his mother had died.

10. Any language study is good mind training while acquiring vocabulary.

11. My farm consisted of about twenty acres of excellent land, having given a hundred pounds for my predecessor's lease.

12. Prepared to encounter a woman of disordered mind, the appearance presented by Mrs. Taylor at his entrance greatly astonished him.

13. Pale and swooning, with two broken legs, they carried him into the house.

14. Count Cassini, the Russian plenipotentiary, had several long and intimate conversations during the tedious weeks of the conference with his British colleague, Sir Arthur Nicholson.

15. But though they had been victorious in the land engagements, they were so little decisive as to lead to no important results.

16. Knowing nothing of the rules of the college or of its customs, it was with the greatest difficulty that the Dean could make me comprehend wherein my wrong-doing lay.

17. Fire, therefore, was the first object of my search. Happily, some embers were found upon the hearth, together with potato-stalks and dry chips. Of these, with much difficulty, I kindled a fire, by which some warmth was imparted to our shivering limbs.

18. In this connection a great deal of historic fact is introduced into the novel about the past history of the cathedral and of Spain.

19. Over the whole scene hung the haze of twilight that is so peaceful.

20. Compared with Italy, living is more expensive.

21. It is a fundamental principle of law to believe a man innocent until he is proved guilty, and once proved guilty, to remain so until proved to the contrary.

22. Not only had the writer entrée to the titled families of Italy in whose villas she was hospitably entertained, but by royalty also.

23. It is not a strange sight to catch a glimpse of deer along the shore.

24. Earnings from other sources are of such a favorable character as to enable a splendid showing to be made by the company.

25. But while earnings have mounted amazingly, the status of affairs is such as to make it impossible to predict the course events may take, with any degree of accuracy.

Get Published!

"Everyone has something they know well or can do well. And when a person has a skill, there's always going to be someone willing to pay for it."

— bnpublishing.com

BN Publishing helps authors publish more titles. So whether you're writing a romance novel, a historical fiction, a mystery, action or suspense story, poetry, about business, a children's book, or any other, we can help you reach your publishing goals.

Besides telling a story, a book is a promotional tool. A book can be likened to a powerful business card since most people won't throw it out. Authoring a book can give you credibility and status, enabling you to charge more for your services.
With our best resources, we will help expose your talent to the public and publish your book for FREE!

Your writing will reach 20,000 retail accounts in the United States (chains, independents, specialty stores, and libraries), including:

www.amazon.com

www.amazon.co.uk

www.amazon.ca

www.bn.com

www.powells.com

www.ebay.com

and more...

Your book will be also included in a physical catalog which goes out to retail stores. Furthermore, when your title is entered into our library, it will automatically appear in bookstore and library databases.

Our United States- and United Kingdom-based sales teams work with clients all over the world through our broad distribution channel partners.

For more information please contact

editor@bnpublishing.com

Recommended Readings

- Think and Grow Rich by Napoleon Hill

- The Master-Key to Riches by Napoleon Hill

- The Law of Success In Sixteen Lessons by Napoleon Hill

- Warren Buffett Talks to MBA Students by Warren Buffett

- How I Learned the Secrets of Success in Selling by Frank Bettger

- You Can Still Make It In The Market by Nicolas Darvas

- The Richest Man in Babylon - Illustrated by George S. Clason

- Show Me Your Options! The Guide to Complete Confidence for Every Stock and Options Trader Seeking Consistent, Predictable Returns By Steve Burns, Christopher Ebert

Available at www.bnpublishing.com

www.ingramcontent.com/pod-product-compliance
Lightning Source LLC
Chambersburg PA
CBHW021426180326
41458CB00001B/152

Figure 1.—OUTER CASE OF ALBANA HARPSICHORD.

Italian Harpsichord Building in the 16th and 17th Centuries

By

John D. Shortridge

CONTRIBUTIONS FROM THE MUSEUM OF HISTORY AND TECHNOLOGY
UNITED STATES NATIONAL MUSEUM BULLETIN 225 · PAPER 15, PAGES 93–107
SMITHSONIAN INSTITUTION PRESS · WASHINGTON, D.C. · 1970

ISBN: 978-1-78139-000-9

Contents

List of Figures

The making of harpsichords flourished in Italy throughout the 16th and 17th centuries. The Italian instruments were of simpler construction than those built by the North Europeans, and they lacked the familiar second manual and array of stops.

In this paper, typical examples of Italian harpsichords from the Hugo Worch Collection in the United States National Museum are described in detail and illustrated. Also, the author offers an explanation for certain puzzling variations in keyboard ranges and vibrating lengths of strings of the Italian harpsichords.

THE AUTHOR: *John D. Shortridge is associate curator of cultural history in the United States National Museum, Smithsonian Institution.*

PERHAPS the modern tendency to idealize progress has been responsible for the neglect of Italian harpsichords and virginals during the present day revival of interest in old musical instruments. Whatever laudable traits the Italian builders may have had, they cannot be considered to have been progressive. Their instruments of the mid-16th century hardly can be distinguished from those made around 1700. During this 150 years the pioneering Flemish makers added the four-foot register, a second keyboard, and lute and buff stops to their instruments. However, the very fact that the Italian builders were unwilling to change their models suggests that their instruments were good enough to demand no further improvements. Anyone who has heard a properly restored Italian harpsichord or an accurately made reproduction will agree that the tone of such instruments is of exceptional beauty.

This paper consists of a description of the structural features of two typical Italian instruments and a general discussion of the stringing and tuning of Italian harpsichords and virginals that is based on certain measurements of 33 instruments housed in various museums in the United States. To the curators and other staff members of these institutions I express my sincere gratitude for making it possible for me to measure valuable instruments entrusted to their care or for supplying similar information by mail.

The first type of instrument described below usually has been designated in modern books about musical instruments and in catalogs of instrument collections as a spinet, the term virginal being applied to the rectangular instruments having the keyboard along the long side. Since both of these types have basically the same arrangement of keyboard, wrest plank, hitch pins, strings and jacks, and since both types were known as virginals in 17th-century England, it is logical to reserve the term spinet for another kind of instrument, namely the one with the wrest plank and tuning pins in front over the keyboard, and with the strings stretched diagonally. Such instruments were popular in England in the late 17th and early 18th centuries and were known in English as spinets during the period of their popularity. By using the term polygonal virginal we can distinguish, when necessary, the five-sided Italian model from the rectangular instruments usually produced in northern Europe. Some rectangular virginals were made in Italy; one Flemish polygonal virginal, made by the elder Hans Ruckers in 1591, survives. Long instruments, resembling the grand piano in shape, are called harpsichords. Of course it is understood that both types of virginals as well as the spinet and the harpsichord were keyed chordophones employing the plucking action of jacks and plectra.

Figure 2.—POLYGONAL VIRGINAL IN OUTER CASE.

Throughout this paper the different octaves are indicated according to the following system:

Figure 3.—POLYGONAL VIRGINAL REMOVED FROM OUTER CASE.

The Typical Italian Polygonal Virginal

To give a clear idea of the construction of the Italian polygonal virginal, a detailed description of one particular example is presented here. This virginal is included in the Hugo Worch collection at the U.S. National Museum. The maker's name is not known, but the instrument is believed to have been built around 1600.

As is true of the great majority of Italian virginals and harpsichords of the 16th and 17th centuries, the instrument proper is removable from its outer case. The outer case (fig. 2), of sturdier construction than the virginal which it was designed to protect, is made of wood about 1/2" thick and is decorated with paintings of female figures and garlands. The original legs are missing.

Our main interest is in the virginal proper (fig. 3), the construction of which is comparable in some ways to that of the violin. The very thin sides of the virginal are held together at the corners by blocks, and the soundboard is supported by a lining.

The cross section drawing (fig. 4) shows the $\frac{9}{16}$" thick bottom and the sides which are $\frac{1}{8}$" thick. The lining, $\frac{1}{2}$" by $1\text{-}\frac{1}{3}$", runs around four sides of the instrument, the wrest plank replacing it on the fifth side. The soundboard thickness, measured inside the holes through which the jacks pass, varies from $\frac{1}{16}$" in the bass to $\frac{1}{8}$" in the treble. The manner in which variations in thickness are distributed over the entire soundboard has not been determined. The cross section drawing also shows the beautifully executed mouldings that make the sides appear to be thicker than they really are.

The positions of the knee braces, the shape of which can be seen in figure 4, are shown along either side of the keyboard in figure 5. These braces are $\frac{3}{4}$" thick. The positions of the blocks, small pieces with the grain running perpendicular to the bottom, and the wrest plank, which is $1\text{-}\frac{1}{4}$" thick, are also shown. The two ribs are attached to the underside of the soundboard in the positions indicated. The jack guide, built up of separate pieces held together by long strips down either side, is glued to the underside of the soundboard and extends as far as the lining in the treble but stops a little short of it in the bass (fig. 5). The jack guide is $^{15}\!/_{16}$" thick.

The layout of the soundboard in figure 6 gives the relative positions of the bridges, tuning pins, hitch pins, strings, jacks, and jack rail. There is, of course, one jack and one string per key. The jacks presently in this virginal, not being original, will not be described. Typical Italian jacks will be described later. The bridges are $^5\!/_{16}$" wide and vary in height from $^7\!/_{16}$" in the bass to $^3\!/_8$" in the treble. A cross section of one of the bridges appears in figure 4. The jack rail, also shown in figure 4, extends over the jacks 1-$^1\!/_8$" above the soundboard. It serves not only to prevent the jacks from flying out during play but also to terminate the downward fall of the fronts of the keys. The keys do not drop far enough to touch the key frame, but instead are stopped by the jacks striking the jack rail.

Figure 4.—CROSS SECTION OF POLYGONAL VIRGINAL. A, side; B, bottom; C, knee; D, liner; E, soundboard; F, rib; G, bridge; H string; I, jack rail. Scale, 1:2.

John D. Shortridge

The keyboard has an apparent compass of four octaves and one note from *E* to *f′′′*. Short octave tuning would have extended the compass down a major third to *C* in the bass, with the *E* key sounding *C*, the *F#* key sounding *D*, the *G#* key sounding *E*, and the remaining keys sounding their proper pitches. These three keys will hereafter be referred to as *C/E, D/F#* and *E/G#*.

The lowest eight keys have small wire eyes attached to their undersides near the front. A corresponding slot is cut through the inner and outer cases, allowing the eyes to be connected to a short pedal keyboard which has not survived.

The keys themselves vary in length from 10" in the bass to 18-$\frac{1}{2}$" in the treble; they are mounted on a trapezoidal key frame which is removable from the instrument. The balance rail and balance rail pins are on a diagonal, resulting in a gradual but noticeable change in the touch from one end of the keyboard to the other. The rack, $\frac{1}{2}$" thick and 1-$\frac{3}{4}$" high, is fastened along the back of the key frame and has one vertical saw cut for each key. Projecting from the back of each key is a small sliver of wood which rides in its proper saw cut and serves to guide the key. The natural keys are veneered with boxwood and have arcaded boxwood fronts. The sharps are small blocks of hardwood stained black.

The sides, soundboard, ribs, jacks, guide, jackrail, and mouldings are made of cypress, the wrest plank and bridges are of walnut, and the framework, bottom, keys, and key frame are of pine.

The photographs (figs. 2, 3) show the decorative use of ivory studs. On the soundboard appears the Latin inscription *Vita brevis, ars longa*. A laminated parchment rose, 3-$\frac{3}{16}$" in diameter, is placed in the soundboard in the position indicated in figure 6. A typical example of this decorative device is shown in figure 12.

The above-described virginal is typical of Italian practice. Other examples studied generally have differed from it only in small details, except in the case of compass and vibrating lengths of strings. These factors will be discussed in detail in a following section.

5

Figure 5.—INTERIOR OF POLYGONAL VIRGINAL. A, lining; B, wrest plank; C, rib; D, jack guide; E, knee; F, rack. Broken lines indicate positions of corner blocks and brace under wrest plank. Scale, 1:8.

Figure 6.—SOUNDBOARD LAYOUT OF POLYGONAL VIRGINAL. Scale, 1:8.

Figure 7.—RIDOLFI HARPSICHORD REMOVED FROM CASE.

Figure 8.—CROSS SECTION OF RIDOLFI HARPSICHORD. A, bottom; B,
knee; C, lining; D, soundboard. Scale, 1:2.

The Typical Italian Harpsichord

The instrument chosen to illustrate the stylistic features of the Italian harpsichord is also in the collection of the U.S. National Museum. This harpsichord, purchased for the Museum in 1892 by Dr. G. Brown Goode, was made in 1665 by Giacomo Ridolfi, who claimed Girolamo Zenti as his teacher. The inscription on the nameboard reads "Jacobus Rodolphus Hieronymi de Zentis Discipulus MDCLXV Facieba."

Like the virginal described above, this harpsichord is separable from its outer case. The outer case rests on a separate stand consisting of three gilt cupids and a floral garland. Since the painted decoration of this case is not original, another outer case, belonging to a harpsichord made by Horatius Albana in 1633, was selected for the illustration (fig. 1).

Two unison strings per key and two registers of jacks are provided. The apparent compass of the keyboard is from C/E to c'''. The remains of pedal connections can be seen on the lowest eight keys.

The sides of the harpsichord are $\frac{5}{32}$" thick; the bottom is $\frac{9}{16}$" thick. The sides and lining are supported by knees that do not extend clear across the bottom of the instrument as they do in the virginal.

The knees are small triangular pieces, as shown in figure 8. Since the added tension of the second set of strings demands a somewhat more substantial framework than that employed in the virginal, a series of braces are attached to the floor. These are connected to the lining by several diagonal braces (fig. 9). This produces a remarkably strong but very light structure. The keys (not shown) are of more constant length than those of the virginal; therefore, the touch is much more uniform.

Figure 9.—FRAMEWORK OF HARPSICHORD. A, wrest plank; B, belly rail; C, rib; D, bottom brace; E, diagonal brace; F, knee; G, lining. Scale, 1:8.

Figure 10.—LAYOUT OF HARPSICHORD SOUNDBOARD. Scale, 1:8.

The wrest plank is supported by two end blocks, against which the partition behind the action (called the belly rail) is also placed. The soundboard is glued to the top of the belly rail. The wrest plank is veneered with cypress, giving the appearance that the soundboard extends over it. The jack guides also rest on the end blocks in the space between the wrest plank and the belly rail. Figures 8 and 11 clarify the arrangement of these structural features.

Figure 10 shows the layout of ribs, bridges, and strings on the soundboard. The soundboard is about $\frac{1}{8}$" thick. The bridge on the wrest plank tapers in height from $\frac{3}{8}$" in the treble to $\frac{7}{16}$" in the bass and in width from $\frac{5}{16}$" to $\frac{7}{16}$". The soundboard bridge measures about $\frac{3}{8}$" by $\frac{1}{4}$" and has virtually no taper. The soundboard does not have a rose, although that decorative device is fairly common on Italian harpsichords.

The jack guides are built up of spacer blocks held together by thin strips along the sides. There is now no provision for moving the guides, although plugged-up holes visible in the right end of each guide suggest that they originally could be disengaged. In Italian harpsichords generally, the jack guides were controlled by knobs projecting through the sides of the case. Sometimes these harpsichords had levers pivoted on the wrest plank and attached to the guides. The Ridolfi case has not been patched and there are no holes in the wrest plank where levers could have been attached; so, the guides probably were not intended to be movable.

The jacks are simple slips of walnut measuring about $\frac{3}{16}$" by $\frac{7}{16}$" by $3\text{-}\frac{1}{8}$". The arrangement of the tongue, spring, plectrum, and damper are shown in figure 11. The dampers are small pieces of buckskin held in slots at the tops of the jacks. The plectra, perhaps not original, are of leather. Of course, there are no adjusting screws or capstans of any variety.

The direction in which the plectra of each row of jacks should be pointing is not known. Two clavicytheria having two registers of strings and a single row of double tongue jacks have been examined by the author. Each of these jacks has two plectra, one pointing to the right and one to the left. Turning these jacks around does not alter the order of direction. The plectra nearest the keyboard points the same way whether the jack is upside down or not. In the clavicytherium at the Smithsonian Institution the plectra nearest the keyboard points to the player's left. In a clavicytherium at the Boston Museum of Fine Arts the opposite is true. Probably both arrangements were used in harpsichords also.

String Lengths and Pitch Standards

The vibrating lengths of the strings of the polygonal virginal and of the Ridolfi harpsichord can be roughly determined from the drawings. For purposes of comparison, a tabulation of the vibrating lengths (in inches) of the *C* strings on both instruments follows:

	Polygonal virginal	*Harpsichord*
c'''	$6\text{-}\frac{5}{8}$	$5\text{-}\frac{1}{16}$
c'' (pitch C)	$12\text{-}\frac{15}{16}$	10
c' (middle C)	$25\text{-}\frac{9}{16}$	$20\text{-}\frac{1}{2}$
c	$43\text{-}\frac{5}{16}$	$42\text{-}\frac{1}{16}$
C/E	$50\text{-}\frac{5}{6}$	$61\text{-}\frac{1}{4}$

The lengths shown for the harpsichord represent the shorter of the two strings with which each key is provided.

In order to produce a uniform tone color throughout the compass of a stringed instrument, it is necessary, among other things, to have the tension of all the strings reasonably uniform. In the treble this is accomplished by varying the string lengths. Since the length of a vibrating string is inversely proportional to its frequency, each string is made about half as long as the string an octave below, two thirds as long as the string a fifth below, etc. This principle cannot be carried all the way into the bass since the lowest strings would be inconveniently long, so somewhere below middle *C* the strings are gradually shortened and the diameters of the wires are increased in compensation.

As the above comparison shows, the string lengths are approximately doubled at each descending octave down to *c'* on the virginal and *c* on the harpsichord. The shape of the case allows the harpsichord to have longer bass strings than the virginal; between *c'* and *c* the string length is doubled in the harpsichord. However, in the virginal the *c* string is considerably less than twice as long as the string an octave above. In fact, the bass strings of the virginal are shortened to such an extent that the lowest string of the harpsichord is much longer than the lowest string of the virginal, although in the treble the virginal has longer strings than the harpsichord.

If the length of one treble string of an instrument of this sort is known, the lengths of all but the bass strings can be readily inferred; we can approximately describe the lengths of two-thirds to three-fourths of the strings of either of the above instruments by giving the length of one string. It has become customary to use *c″* for this purpose, and to refer to it in such cases as pitch *C*.

In examining a number of Italian harpsichords and virginals dating from 1540 to 1694, lengths for pitch *C* ranging from 8" to 13-¾" have been found. This seems to be a great discrepancy for instruments that are otherwise so standardized. Since a uniform standard of pitch did not yet exist in the 16th and 17th centuries, we would expect the string lengths employed to be varied somewhat in order to accommodate the instruments to higher or lower tunings. Also, a preference for the sound of thinner, longer wires or shorter, thicker ones may have caused some builders to increase or decrease the string lengths on their instruments in proportion to the string diameters chosen. We have no precise evidence concerning the original wire gauges of the strings of Italian harpsichords and virginals. Although the variety of pitch *C* lengths encountered on the instruments studied can partially be accounted for by these two factors, a third and more important cause existed.

Among the 33 instruments about which information has been secured, a correlation is discernible between the apparent manual compass and the pitch *C* string lengths. Sixteen of the instruments ascend to *f‴*. For these, the length of the pitch *C* string varies from 10-¼" to 13-¾". The remaining instruments, with either *a″* or *c‴* as the highest notes, have pitch *C* strings ranging from 8" to 11-⅜" in length. If the average tension and wire diameter of the two groups are assumed to have been about equal, the difference in string lengths would suggest a corresponding difference in pitch, the instruments having the compass extended to *f‴* sounding somewhat lower than the others.

John D. Shortridge

Figure 11.—ACTION OF HARPSICHORD. A, bottom; B, belly rail; C, soundboard; D, wrest plank; E, key frame; F, rack; G, key; H, jack; I, jack rail. Scale, 1:2.

There is some historical evidence that this actually was the case. In his *Theatrum Instrumentorum* Michael Praetorius[1] pictures a polygonal virginal, which appears to be very much like the many Italian examples that survive today, and a rectangular virginal that seems to be Flemish. He specifies that both are *so recht Chor-Thon* (at regular choir pitch). Praetorius also shows a harpsichord[2] that looks like a typical Italian instrument except for the presence of a set of strings tuned an octave above unison pitch, a rare feature on Italian harpsichords. This harpsichord is described as *so eine Quart tieffer alss Chor-Thon* (a fourth lower than choir pitch), clearly indicating that single manual keyboard instruments a fourth apart in pitch were in existence. Since no reason is given for the harpsichord being tuned a fourth lower than the two virginals, we may assume that the author considered the matter commonplace enough as to demand no further elaboration and that instruments a fourth apart in pitch were not rare.

Praetorius does not state that the harpsichord in his illustration was tuned to a low pitch standard, which was actually used for certain purposes or in particular localities. He discussed the numerous pitches in use before and during his time, but the only one that he mentioned as being a fourth below choir pitch he considered obsolete and suitable only for plainsong. If the harpsichord was not intended to be tuned to

---

[1] Michael Praetorius, Theatrum Instrumentorum, Wolfenbüttel, 1620, pl. 14.
[2] Ibid., pl. 6.

13

this standard and used for this purpose, it must have been tuned to choir pitch and treated as a transposing instrument.

Querinus van Blankenburg,[1] writing in 1739, states:

> At that time [the beginning of the 17th century], men had so little experience in transposition that in order to be able to transpose a piece a fourth downwards they made a special second keyboard in the harpsichord for this purpose. This seems incredible, but the very remarkable proof is the fact that the famous Ruckers from the beginning of the last century for a period of more than thirty years made harpsichords only in this way.[2]

That the second manual of the two-manual harpsichord originated as a device for transposition is well known. In an article titled "Transposing Keyboards on Extant Flemish Harpsichords," Sibyl Marcuse[3] discusses surviving examples that show how the second keyboard was arranged. The upper keyboard was the principal one, with the lower keyboard sounding a fourth below. The strings acted upon by a *c* key on the upper manual were sounded by an *f* key on the lower; so, in changing from the upper manual to the lower, the player would have to move his hands to the left the distance of a perfect fourth in order to strike the same keys, thus producing the downward transposition. The compass of the upper manual was *E/C* to *c'''*. Since the lower keyboard was shifted to the left, space was provided for five additional keys at its treble end. The apparent treble range of the lower keyboard was therefore extended to *f'''*, although the lower *f'''* and upper *c'''* keys worked on the same strings and produced the same pitch. Room was also made for five extra bass keys at the lower end of the upper manual. However, since short octave tuning was employed and it was desirable to be able to use the same fingering in the bass on both manuals, the tails of the *C/E*, *D/F#* and *E/G#* keys of the upper manual had to be bent to the left in order to work on the strings played by the *F*, *G*, and *A* keys respectively of the lower manual. The vacant space to the left of the upper manual *C/E* was filled by a block of wood. Hence the

---

[1] Querinus van Blankenburg, Elementa Musica, The Hague, 1739.
[2] Translation by Arthur Mendel in "Devices for Transposition in the Organ before 1600," Acta Musicologica, 1949, p. 33.
[3] Sibyl Marcuse, "Transposing Keyboards on Extant Flemish Harpsichords," Musical Quarterly, July 1952.

five extra bass strings not used by the upper manual were those played by the *C/E*, *D/F#*, *E/G#*, *B*, and *c#* keys of the lower keyboard.

Of the 16 Italian harpsichords and virginals studied that ascend in the treble to f''', 13 range to *C/E* in the bass, thus having exactly the same compass as the lower (transposing) keyboard of the Flemish two-manual instruments. Twelve of the 14 Italian examples having c''' as the highest key stop on *C/E* in the bass and are identical in apparent compass to the Ruckers upper manual.

The correlation of compass and string length of the Italian instruments, the statements of Praetorius, and the similarity of the Italian keyboard ranges to those of the Ruckers transposing harpsichords have been considered. A plausible conclusion is that the Italian instruments extending to f''' were transposing instruments sounding a perfect fourth lower than the prevailing pitch standard. Adopting the terminology used for orchestral wind instruments, these could be referred to as harpsichords in *G*.

The evidence of the correlation between string length and compass becomes much more convincing if we assume that the Italian builders abandoned the practice of making transposing harpsichords about the same time that the Ruckers family stopped employing the transposing lower manual. In the quotation previously given, Querinus van Blankenburg tells us that the Ruckers did not make transposing instruments later than the 1630's. Of the 10 dated Italian instruments with the keyboard extended to f''', only three were made after the third decade of the 17th century. Each of these has a shorter pitch *C* string than any of the seven earlier instruments. These three harpsichords, dated 1654, 1658, and 1666, are accordingly considered nontransposing instruments, with the extra treble keys representing an actual extension of the upward range. The six undated instruments with f''' in the treble are classified as transposing instruments because of their pitch *C* lengths and are accordingly believed to have been made before about 1635.

The 33 instruments on which this study is based are classified in the list on page 107. They are grouped according to whether the highest key is f''' or c''', with the exceptions of the three harpsichords mentioned in the preceding paragraph and three instruments that go only to a''. That the three instruments ending on a'' belong with the nontransposing group is indicated by their string lengths.

The listing gives additional information about each example. String lengths of instruments having two registers are for the shorter of the two pitch *C* strings.

Figure 12.—TYPICAL DECORATIVE DEVICE, known as rose, that appeared in soundboards of virginals and harpsichords.

Information has been secured on two Italian virginals which were not included in the tabulation. Their measurements are completely at variance with the pattern consistently set by the other 33 examples studied. One, made by Giovanni Domenico in 1556, is in the Skinner collection; it has a pitch C string 14-$\frac{1}{16}$" in length and an apparent compass of C/E to c'''. The other, with the same apparent compass and a 7-$\frac{1}{2}$" pitch C string, is at Yale University. Whether these instruments are exceptional in terms of the pitch to which they were tuned, the tension which was applied to the strings, or the thickness and weight of the strings themselves, has not been determined.

The average of the pitch C lengths of the transposing instruments in the list is 12.78"; that of the nontransposing group is 10.45". This suggests a separation between the two groups of about a major third since the first average is roughly $\frac{5}{4}$ of the second. However, the fact that the

16

separation of the two averages is not great enough to positively indicate a perfect fourth—the first average would have to be $\frac{4}{3}$ of the
second to do so—does not disprove the theory of transposition by a
fourth. In the first place, a considerable variety of pitches is no doubt
represented in both groups since a universal pitch standard did not exist in the 16th and 17th centuries. Also, a margin of error of only a
semitone is as good as could be expected considering the small number of examples on which the averages are based.

A further possible justification for the relationship of the two averages is found in Praetorius' discussion of the pitch standards with
which he was familiar.[1] He states that choir pitch was a major second
lower than chamber pitch and that *tertiam minorem* was a minor third
lower than chamber pitch. Praetorius says of *tertiam minorem*:[2]

> But in Italy and in various Catholic choirs in Germany,
> the said lower pitch is much in use. For some Italians, not
> unjustly, take no pleasure in high singing, and maintain it
> is not beautiful, and the words cannot be properly under-
> stood, and it sounds like crowing, yelling, singing at the
> top of one's voice....

Possibly some of the nontransposing instruments were tuned to
choir pitch and others to *tertiam minorem*, while the transposing instruments were set a fourth lower than choir pitch.

Three of the instruments listed are ottavinas, small instruments
tuned an octave higher than usual. Ottavinas correspond to a four-foot
register. Mersenne[3] mentions that they existed in two sizes, one a fifth
above the usual pitch and the other an octave above. The three ottavinas included in the table are considered to be of the size sounding
an octave above the usual pitch because they have *C/E* to *c'''* ranges
and pitch *C* string lengths about half the average length of the other
instruments in the nontransposing group. Although no examples were
found for inclusion in this study, it is probable that some ottavinas a
fifth above the usual pitch—and therefore an octave higher than the
transposing instruments in our listing—survive. Such instruments

---

[1] Michael Praetorius, Syntagma Musicum, Wolfenbüttel, 1614–1620, vol. 2
(Organographia), chapter 2.
[2] Translation by Arthur Mendel in "Pitch in the 16th and early 17th Centuries,
Part II," Musical Quarterly, April 1948.
[3] Marin Mersenne, Harmonie Universelle, Paris, 1636, p. 101.

would be expected to have apparent ranges of *C/E* to *f‴* and pitch *C* strings between 5-$\frac{3}{4}$" and 6-$\frac{3}{4}$" in length.

DATA ON THE 33 INSTRUMENTS STUDIED

Date	Pitch C length (*in inches*)	Apparent compass	Type	Reg- isters	Maker	Present Location
			TRANSPOSING INSTRUMENTS			
1540	11-$\frac{11}{16}$	C/E-f″	Polygonal virginal	8′	Vi ... ies	Metropolitan Museum of Art
1569	13-$\frac{1}{4}$	C/E-f‴	Polygonal virginal	8′	Annibale Rossi	Juilliard School of Music
1602	13-$\frac{1}{4}$	C/E-f‴	Rectangu-lar virginal	8′	Ioannes Baptista Bononien	Smithsonian Institution
1610	13-$\frac{1}{2}$	C/E-f‴′	Polygonal virginal	8′	Pasquino Querci	Harding Museum, Chi-cago
1613	11-$\frac{1}{2}$	C/E-f‴	Harpsi-chord	8′8′	Pasquino Querci	Smithsonian Insitution
1617	13-$\frac{3}{4}$	C/E-f‴	Polygonal virginal	8′	Giovanni Battista Boni	Yale University, New Haven, Conn.
1620	13-$\frac{9}{16}$	C/E-f‴	Polygonal virginal	8′	Frances-co Poggio	Rhode Island School of Design, Providence
	11-$\frac{15}{16}$	C/E-f‴	Polygonal virginal	8′	Anony-mous	Skinner Collection, Holyoke, Mass.
	12-$\frac{15}{16}$	C/E-f‴	Polygonal virginal	8′	Anony-mous	Smithsonian Institution

18

Date	Pitch C length (*in inches*)	Apparent compass	Type	Reg- isters	Maker	Present Location
	13"	C/E-f‴	Polygonal virginal	8′	Anony- mous	Boston Museum of Fine Arts
	11-½	C-f‴	Polygonal virginal	8′	Anony- mous	Folger Library, Washington, D.C.
	12-¾	C/E-f‴	Polygonal virginal	8′	Anony- mous	Cincinnati Art Museum
	13-⅝	C/E-f‴	Polygonal virginal	8′	Anony- mous	Smithsonian Institution

NONTRANSPOSING INSTRUMENTS

Date	Pitch C length	Apparent compass	Type	Reg- isters	Maker	Present Location
1548	11	C/E-c‴	Polygonal virginal	8′	Domenicus Pesauren- sis	Metropolitan Museum of Art
1554	[1]10-½	C/E-c‴	Harpsi- chord	8′8′	Padre Stoppacio	Vassar College, Poughkeep- sie, New York
1585	[2]11-½	C/E-a″	Ottavina	4′	Franciscus Bonafinis	Metropolitan Museum of Art

---

[1] This length is approximate. It is double the length of the shortest string on the instrument. .

[2] In order to arrive at a meaningful average value for the string lengths of the nontransposing group, it was necessary to double the measured lengths of the pitch C strings of the three instruments tuned an octave higher. .

19

Italian Harpsichord Building in the 16th and 17th Centuries

Date	Pitch C length (*in inches*)	Apparent compass	Type	Registers	Maker	Present Location
1602	10-$\frac{1}{2}$	C/E-c$'''$	Harpsichord	......	Christoforus Rigunini	Stearns Collection, Ann Arbor, Mich.
1615	[1]9-$\frac{3}{4}$	C/E-a$''$	Ottavina	4$'$	Pasquino Querci	Metropolitan Museum of Art
1625	10-$\frac{1}{8}$	C/E-c$'''$	Harpsichord	8$'$	Valerius Peres	Skinner Collection, Holyoke, Mass.
1633	11-$\frac{3}{8}$	C/E-c$'''$	Harpsichord	8$'$8$'$	Horatius Albana	Smithsonian Instituion
1645	11	C/E-c$'''$	Harpsichord	8$'$8$'$	Horatius Albana	Vizcaya, Miami, Fla.
1654	10-$\frac{1}{4}$	C/E-f$'''$	Harpsichord	8$'$8$'$	Anonymous	Smithsonian Institution
1658	11-$\frac{1}{8}$	C-f$''$	Harpsichord	8$'$8$'$	Hieronymus de Zentis	Metropolitan Museum of Art
1665	10	C/E-c$'''$	Harpsichord	8$'$8$'$	Giacomo Ridolfi	Smithsonian Institution
1666	10-$\frac{15}{16}$	A_1-f$''$	Harpsichord	8$'$8$'$	Hieronymus de Zentis	Metropolitan Museum of Art

---

[1] In order to arrive at a meaningful average value for the string lengths of the nontransposing group, it was necessary to double the measured lengths of the pitch C strings of the three instruments tuned an octave higher. .

Date	Pitch C length (*in inches*)	Apparent compass	Type	Registers	Maker	Present Location
1682	10-⅞	C/E-c'''	Harpsi-chord	8'8'	Giacomo Ridolfi	Rhode Island School of Design, Providence
1683	8	C/E-c'''	Polygonal virginal	8'	B. Obici	Harding Museum, Chicago
1690	10-13/16	C/E-c'''	Harpsi-chord	8'	Giovanni Andrea Menegoni	Smithsonian Institution
1693	10-5/16	G1-c'''	Harpsi-chord	8'8'	Anony-mous	Smithsonian Institution
1694	9-⅞	C-c''' (minus C#)	Harpsi-chord	8'8' 4'	Nicolaus de Quoco	Smithsonian Institution
	9-¾	C/E-a''	Clavicytherium	8'8'	Anony-mous	Smithsonian Institution
	[1]10-⅜	C/E-c'''	Clavicytherium (Ottavina)	4'	Anony-mous	Boston Museum of Fine Arts
	11	C/E-c'''	Polygonal virginal	8'	Anony-mous	Smithsonian Institution

---

[1] In order to arrive at a meaningful average value for the string lengths of the nontransposing group, it was necessary to double the measured lengths of the pitch C strings of the three instruments tuned an octave higher. .

Italian Harpsichord Building in the 16th and 17th Centuries

Figure	Negative Number	Catalog Number
1	56322	326,905
2	46792	303,544
3	49355A	303,544
4	49355B	303,544
5	49356A	303,544
6	49356	303,544
7	49356D	332,173
8	49356D	332,173
9	49357A	332,173
10	49357	332,173
11	49355C	332,173
12	46795	303,545

Storia di un'anima - in Italian
Ambrogio Bazzero
Benediction Classics, 2011
250 pages
ISBN: 978-1-84902-287-3

Available from www.amazon.com, www.amazon.co.uk

Storia di un'anima (Story of a Soul) was written by Ambrogio Bazzero, but was first published posthumously by Emilio De Marchi in 1885, with a long preface describing the life and works of Bazzero. The book collects, in the form of diary, the confessions of a sensitive soul and it has a melancholy romantic feeling. This book is available only in Italian

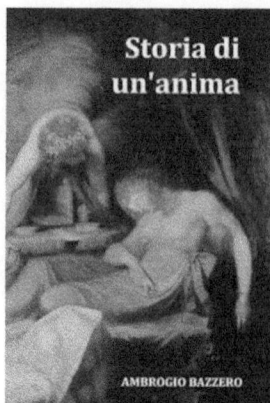

From Ritual to Romance
Jessie L. Weston
Benediction Classics, 2011
188 pages
ISBN: 978-1-84902-415-0

Available from www.amazon.com, www.amazon.co.uk

From Ritual to Romance was written in 1920 by Jessie L. Weston. The book was made famous by being mentioned by T. S. Eliot in the notes to his poem, The Waste Land. He says, "Not only the title, but the plan and a good deal of the incidental symbolism of the poem were suggested by Miss Jessie L. Weston's book". The book centres on an examination of the roots of the King Arthur legends and seeks to make connections between the early pagan elements and the later Christian influences. In particular, the book looks at the Holy Grail tradition and its influence.

The Borgias
One of the Celebrated Crimes stories
Alexandre Dumas, Pere
Benediction Classics, 2011
198 pages
ISBN: 978-1-84902-437-2

Available from www.amazon.com, www.amazon.co.uk

The 'Borgias' is the first volume if the 'Celebrated Crimes' series, written by Alexandre Dumas, Pere, prior writing his well known of historical novels. His works show an intimate knowledge of the characters, and they are written without sparing the details. The subjects are of historical importance and show the semi-lawlessness that was typical of Europe in the Middle Ages. The 'Celebrated Crimes' series were an instant hit and Dumas was inundated with suggestions of other celebrated criminals to write about. The stories continue to astonish readers today.

The Gracchi Marius and Sulla Epochs Of Ancient History - with original maps and sidenotes as sub headings
A. H. Beesley
Benediction Classics, 2011
178 pages
ISBN: 978-1-84902-417-4

Available from www.amazon.com, www.amazon.co.uk

Epochs of ancient history, the Gracchi, Marius and Sulla was written by A.H. Beesley in 1921. It is a historical text, describing a time of crisis in the Roman Empire, which eventually culminated in its demise. Beesley sought to provide the most a consistent and faithful account of the leaders and legislation of this era. He drew on Long's 'History of the Decline of the Roman Republic' and Mommsen's 'History of Rome'. This edition comes complete with the original maps and the sidenotes have been converted into subheadings.

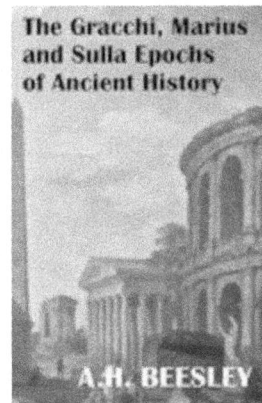

Also from Benediction Books …
Wandering Between Two Worlds: Essays on Faith and Art
Anita Mathias
Benediction Books, 2007
152 pages
ISBN: 0955373700

Available from www.amazon.com, www.amazon.co.uk

In these wide-ranging lyrical essays, Anita Mathias writes, in lush, lovely prose, of her naughty Catholic childhood in Jamshedpur, India; her large, eccentric family in Mangalore, a sea-coast town converted by the Portuguese in the sixteenth century; her rebellion and atheism as a teenager in her Himalayan boarding school, run by German missionary nuns, St. Mary's Convent, Nainital; and her abrupt religious conversion after which she entered Mother Teresa's convent in Calcutta as a novice. Later rich, elegant essays explore the dualities of her life as a writer, mother, and Christian in the United States-- Domesticity and Art, Writing and Prayer, and the experience of being "an alien and stranger" as an immigrant in America, sensing the need for roots.

About the Author

Anita Mathias is the author of *Wandering Between Two Worlds: Essays on Faith and Art*. She has a B.A. and M.A. in English from Somerville College, Oxford University, and an M.A. in Creative Writing from the Ohio State University, USA. Anita won a National Endowment of the Arts fellowship in Creative Nonfiction in 1997. She lives in Oxford, England with her husband, Roy, and her daughters, Zoe and Irene.

Anita's website:
    http://www.anitamathias.com, and
Anita's blog Dreaming Beneath the Spires:
    http://dreamingbeneaththespires.blogspot.com

The Church That Had Too Much
Anita Mathias
Benediction Books, 2010
52 pages
ISBN: 9781849026567

Available from www.amazon.com, www.amazon.co.uk

The Church That Had Too Much was very well-intentioned. She
wanted to love God, she wanted to love people, but she was both ham-
pered by her muchness and the abundance of her possessions, and
beset by ambition, power struggles and snobbery. Read about the sur-
prising way The Church That Had Too Much began to resolve her
problems in this deceptively simple and enchanting fable.

About the Author

Anita Mathias is the author of *Wandering Between Two Worlds: Essays on Faith and Art*. She has a B.A. and M.A. in English from
Somerville College, Oxford University, and an M.A. in Creative Writing from the Ohio State University, USA. Anita won a National
Endowment of the Arts fellowship in Creative Nonfiction in 1997.
She lives in Oxford, England with her husband, Roy, and her daughters, Zoe and Irene.

Anita's website:
    http://www.anitamathias.com, and
Anita's blog Dreaming Beneath the Spires:
    http://dreamingbeneaththespires.blogspot.com

www.ingramcontent.com/pod-product-compliance
Lightning Source LLC
Chambersburg PA
CBHW021426180326
41458CB00001B/153